MW01627584

ArtScroll® Youth Series

Rabbi Nosson Scherman / Rabbi Gedaliah Zlotowitz

General Editors

Rabbi Meir Zlotowitz ז״ל, *Founder*

Action Park
AUGUST 2021
Published by
ARTSCROLL®
Mesorah Publications, ltd

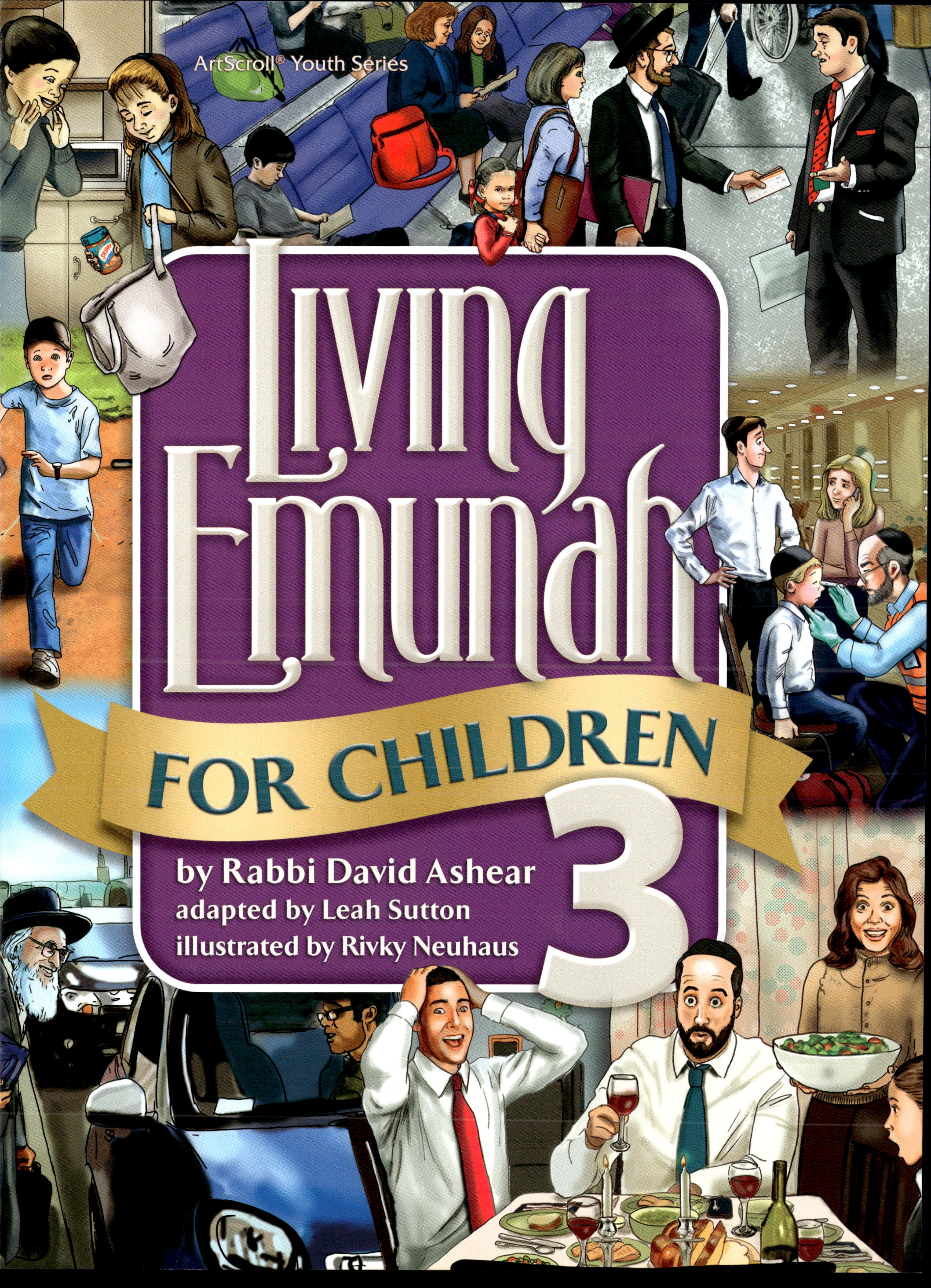

ArtScroll® Youth Series
Living Emunah
FOR CHILDREN
3
by Rabbi David Ashear
adapted by Leah Sutton
illustrated by Rivky Neuhaus

"LIVING EMUNAH FOR CHILDREN 3"

First edition – First impression: November 2022

Published by **MESORAH PUBLICATIONS, LTD.**
313 Regina Avenue / Rahway, N.J 07065 / (718) 921-9000 / Fax: (718) 680-1875
www.artscroll.com

Illustrated by Rivky Neuhaus.

Distributed in Israel by **SIFRIATI / A. GITLER**
POB 2351 / Bnei Brak 51122 / Israel / 03-579-8187

Distributed in Europe by **LEHMANNS**
Unit E, Viking Business Park, Rolling Mill Road / Jarrow, Tyne and Wear / England NE32 3DP

Distributed in Australia and New Zealand by **GOLDS WORLD OF JUDAICA**
3-13 William Street / Balaclava, Melbourne 3183 / Victoria, Australia

Distributed in South Africa by **KOLLEL BOOKSHOP**
Northfield Centre / 17 Northfield Avenue / Glenhazel 2192 / Johannesburg, South Africa

Printed in PRC

ISBN-10: 1-4226-3226-1
ISBN-13: 978-1-4226-3226-0

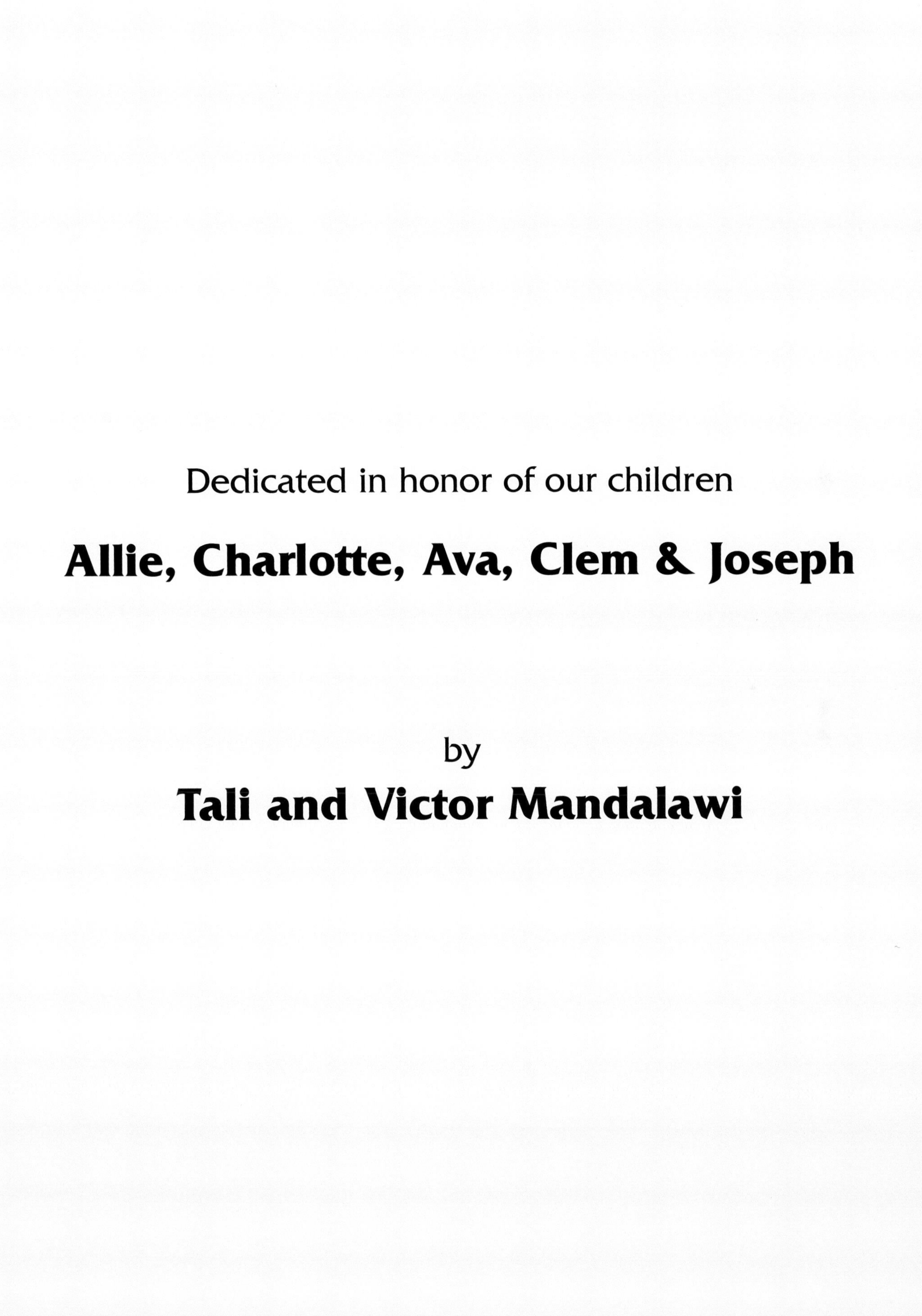

Dedicated in honor of our children

Allie, Charlotte, Ava, Clem & Joseph

by

Tali and Victor Mandalawi

I would like to thank **Hashem** for guiding this project throughout.

A special thanks to the people who worked hard to bring it to reality: **Rabbi David Sutton** for coordinating this project; **Leah Sutton** for choosing and adapting the stories from *Living Emunah*; **Rabbi Nosson Scherman** for his editorial input; **Rivky Neuhaus** for her delightful illustrations that make the stories come alive; **Chanie Ziegler** for the beautiful page layout and **Eli Kroen** for the magnificent cover design; **Mendy Herzberg** and the entire **ArtScroll team;** lastly, the generous sponsors. Thank you to **Tali and Victor Mandalawi,** for graciously dedicating this book. May Hashem bless you with the strength to continue all of your hard work on behalf of our community. May this book be accepted by the public and inspire children to a life of Emunah.

Rabbi David Ashear

Table of Contents

A Joyous Shabbos

One Shabbos, the chassidim of the Baal Shem Tov noticed their Rebbe smiling a lot.

"What is it, Rebbe?" his chassid Yaakov Yosef asked.

"I will tell you after Shabbos," came the reply.

They waited curiously. After Shabbos, the Baal Shem Tov took a few of his close chassidim on a short walk. They stopped in front of a small home.

"What is this all about?" Yechiel Michel asked.

"You'll see," replied the Baal Shem Tov. "Just come with me."

They knocked on the door. "Come in, come in," Shabsai, the home-owner invited. "Have a seat. Why do we deserve such a special visit?" he asked.

They entered and looked around. The house was sparkling clean, and a man and his wife looked at them with big smiles. It was obvious that the couple didn't have a family. There were no signs of children or bottles or mess anywhere.

"Something happened this Shabbos," the Baal Shem Tov said. "Please tell us about it."

Shabsai blushed, but he did as the Baal Shem Tov requested.

"At our wedding, my wife, Perel, and I both said that we would always try to be happy, no matter what. And we've managed to do that for twenty years. But this Shabbos it was harder than usual. You see, we live very simply. We save some money each week to buy food for Shabbos. This week, we had no money for food. I told my wife, 'We don't have food and we don't have children, but we still have our simchah. Let's try to be happy this Shabbos anyway.

“I told her to boil a pot of water l’kavod Shabbos. When Shabbos arrived, and we sat down for our seudah, she brought out bowls of water for us. We tried our best to imagine that we were eating like on any other Shabbos. We sipped a spoonful of the water and said, ‘Mmm! This tastes just like delicious Shabbos fish!’ We were so happy and grateful to Hashem, that we began to sing thanks to Him.

“I told my wife, ‘Bring out the chicken soup!’ She brought out two bowls of water. We each took a spoonful, and imagined that it tasted just like our usual Shabbos food! We were overjoyed! Once again, we sang and thanked Hashem for the many blessings He has given us. We kept doing this, until we had some water for a delicious dessert.”

Shabsai looked at the Baal Shem Tov and said, “We never experienced so much joy in our lives! We feel so close to Hashem!”

The chassidim were astonished. The couple had no children and no money, yet they were was so happy!

The Baal Shem Tov’s eyes filled with tears. “What you did brought Hashem so much joy. Hashem loves you so much, and He wants to bring *you* joy now, too. With Hashem’s help, by this time next year, you will have a son. He will light up the world with Torah, and bring you lots of happiness!”

Sure enough, one year later, Shabsai and Perel Hopstein had a beautiful baby boy. They named him Yisrael after the Baal Shem Tov. He grew up to be the great Maggid of Kozhnitz.

Hashem loves when we can recognize that everything He does is with so much love. It’s easier for us to face a challenge when we know that.

A Kiss on the Forehead

R' Yitzchak Dovid Grossman is a special person. He not only heads a large institution but also travels from Eretz Yisrael to America to collect money for Midgal Ohr. Migdal Ohr is an organization that provides schools and homes for orphans and poor children.

This story happened to Rabbi Grossman on one trip to America.

As he reached the gate to board a plane, one of the flight attendants recognized him. "Rabbi Grossman," he said respectfully, "would you like to be moved to first class, free of charge? I do it for special customers," he said with a wink.

Rabbi Grossman smiled. "I usually don't agree to sit in first class because I don't want anyone to think that I am using the money they have donated for my own comfort or luxuries. But today I am not feeling so well; I think I will take you up on your offer."

As he settled into his comfortable seat, he noticed an elderly American couple seated across from him. "Hello, my name is Yitzchak Dovid Grossman," he introduced himself. "It's nice to meet you. I raise money for a place called Migdal Ohr. Would you like to see a video of the things we do in this organization?"

The couple nodded agreeably, but Rabbi Grossman was surprised with himself. *I've never done this before,* he thought to himself. *I don't know what came over me.*

He set his laptop on the tray in front of them, and the video began to play. When it was finished, they looked up, impressed.

"It seems like a wonderful organization," the man said.

"Thank you," Rabbi Grossman answered as he leaned over to take his laptop.

SLAM!

Rabbi Grossman looked up; horrified. As he was reaching over to take his laptop, his arm had pressed a button on the elderly man's armrest, causing the back to fall flat.

"I am so, so sorry," Rabbi Grossman apologized, embarrassed. He quickly helped him sit up and then kissed the man's forehead before returning to his seat.

What was that about? he wondered to himself. *First the introductions, and now the kiss! What has come over me today? This is so unlike me!* Rabbi Grossman kept his head down, embarrassed. Five minutes later, there was a tap on his shoulder. It was the elderly man!

"I love Israel, and I love the Jewish people even more," the man began. "I had decided that I was going to make a big donation to an organization that helps needy children, but I did not know which one to choose. I told my wife, 'The first person who shows me a program that benefits children and kisses me on the forehead, will get my donation!'"

Right there, the man pulled out a check for a great deal of money and handed to Rabbi Grossman.

Rabbi Grossman was stunned. Migdal Ohr was in the midst of building a new home for needy girls and they had no idea how they were going to pay for it. He thanked the man, and he thanked Hashem.

There's always a reason why we do or say something. We might think, "Why did I offer to help? I really don't have the time," or, "Why did I go over to that parent to say Mazel Tov? I am so shy." We may not know it at that moment, but we know Hashem had us do it for a reason.

Warmed Through

It was Elul; the year was 1930. Rav Yechezkel Abramsky was the rav of Slutzk, Belarus, which was part of the Soviet Union. He taught Torah and wrote sefarim. The Communist government tried to stop the Jews from doing mitzvos and learning Torah.

Rav Yechezkel Abramsky knew what he had to do. No matter how frightening it was, he kept teaching and learning Torah!

Knock, knock! Bang, bang!

The Soviet police had come to Rav Abramsky's home to arrest him.. Rav Yechezkel knew that Hashem would protect him. The only thing that Rav Yechezkel feared was the cold. You see, anyone who was caught keeping or teaching mitzvos was sent to freezing cold Siberia.

Rav Yechezkel was sensitive to cold. All his life, from when he was a young child, he would wear many layers of clothing to protect himself from becoming sick. But what would protect him in Siberia?

As expected, Rav Yechezkel was found guilty and sentenced to Siberia.

"You're going to spend five years here, so get comfortable!" the Russian soldier laughed when they reached Siberia. "Now take off your coat! And your shirt, and your socks, and your shoes. We're going to see how well you can walk on ice."

Rav Abramsky knew he had to do what he had been ordered if he wanted any chance of remaining alive.

"Hashem," he davened, "the Gemara tells us that everything is in Your hands, except if someone exposes himself to very hot or very cold temperatures. The Torah commands us to take care of our health. If someone goes outside without a coat and becomes sick, it is his own fault. But now, I have no choice. I am forced to work outside in the cold without enough clothing. So, this time, it's not in my hands. It's in *Your* hands. Please, Hashem, protect me from the cold."

Miraculously, after only a year in Siberia, the Communists let him leave. The weeks and months that he spent there were very hard, but Rav Yechezkel Abramsky never caught a cold even once.

We must do whatever we can to protect ourselves. But once we've done our best, we daven to Hashem. Hashem will take care of us from then on.

Six-year-old Yitzchak coughed loudly as his mother pressed a wet cloth to his forehead.

"Oy, Yitzchak," she sighed. "May Hashem have rachmanus and send you a refuah sheleimah."

"Amen," Yitzchak's father, Dov, replied. "Perel, you go take a rest. I'll stay with Yitzchak."

Perel Scheiner tiredly made her way to her bed as her husband stroked their son's back.

"Yitzchak," he said softly, "so many people are davening for you to get better. Many people have even taken on kabbalos to improve in a certain mitzvah, but you haven't accepted anything on yourself."

Yitzchak opened his eyes. "Me?" he asked weakly. "What do you think I should do? There isn't much I can do while lying in bed."

"A kabbalah doesn't have to be something that you can do right now. It can be for the future.

"You're young, and you don't yet have to daven with a minyan. Why don't you accept upon yourself that when you are better you'll always daven Shacharis with a minyan? B'ezras Hashem, you will have a refuah sheleimah, and you will be able to keep that kabbalah for your whole life."

Yitzchak agreed, and soon had a refuah sheleimah.

Years passed, and Yitzchak kept his kabbalah for almost seventy years. Eventually, he became known as the Rosh Yeshivah of Kaminetz in Yerushalayim, the great Rav Yitzchak Scheiner!

The yeshivah needed money, and Rav Yitzchak decided to travel to America to raise the funds needed. When it was time to return home, he called his travel agent.

EH-

"I am going to need a minyan for Shacharis on the plane," he explained.

"I cannot guarantee that there will be a minyan on the plane," the travel agent replied. "But I can book a flight that will stop off in Amsterdam, where you can try to find a minyan for Shacharis. Then, you can travel from Amsterdam to Eretz Yisrael. The trip will be longer, and more expensive."

Rav Yitzchak told the travel agent to book those flights.

His first flight to Amsterdam landed at 8 a.m., as planned.

"Hashem," he davened, "I don't know the people here, I don't know the language here, I don't know the streets here. All I know is that in the last 70 years I didn't miss davening Shacharis with a minyan even once. Please, lead me to the right place."

He left the terminal and walked to the curb. Less than two minutes later, a car pulled up alongside him. There was a Jewish man in the driver's seat.

"Would you like to help me make a minyan for Shacharis?" he called through the window.

Rav Yitzchak happily accepted, and they made their way to a small shul to daven.

After davening, the man turned to Rav Yitzchak. "Where are you headed?"

"I feel bad to ask," Rav Yitzchak replied, "but I need to make it back to the airport."

"No problem," the man replied. "I'm a taxi driver, and I was heading back there, too."

Rav Yitzchak made it to the airport with just enough time for his flight!

When he returned to the yeshivah, he told this story to his students. "When you accept a mitzvah upon yourself, don't worry! If it gets too hard, Hashem will carry you."

A Simple Jar of Peanut Butter

Esther and Avner were one of many newly married couples living in Yerushalayim. They had moved from Montreal, Canada, shortly after their wedding. They loved the land. Avner loved davening at the Kosel on most mornings, and Esther loved walking through the old streets and the vibrant shuks. But, sometimes, they missed home. They missed their families and the small conveniences that they enjoyed in Montreal.

One day, when Esther was in the supermarket, she saw a jar of peanut butter. *Ooh, this is like the peanut butter I used to spread on my bread,* she thought longingly. She put the jar in her cart and took it home.

That afternoon, Esther was quietly laughing to herself. *Who knew that having a peanut butter sandwich for lunch could be so exciting?!*

As she tore off the foil from the top of the jar, she noticed that although this brand of peanut butter was familiar, the hashgachah was not. "I'll call Tatty; he's a mashgiach at a food plant. He'll surely know if it's good."

Rabbi Herskowitz was very happy to hear from his daughter. When he heard her question, he shook his head. "It's better not to use that peanut butter," he said gently.

Esther thanked him and hung up the phone. She tossed the jar into the trash can and sighed. "It's just a silly jar of peanut butter," she told

SKIPPY
CREAMY
SKIPPY

herself. "No need to get so upset." But that didn't help. It just made her feel even worse.

Suddenly, Esther heard knocking on her apartment door. *Who can it be*? she thought. *We hardly know anyone here.*

She opened the door, and there was Chaya, her cousin from Montreal who had come to Eretz Yisrael on vacation!

"Chaya!" she exclaimed, giving her a big hug. "So good to see you!" The two cousins chatted for a few minutes, and then Chaya picked up her bag.

"Your mother heard I was coming to Eretz Yisrael and she wanted to send you something. She went racing all through the house looking for something you would like, but it was last minute. Finally, she decided to send you *this*!" Chaya laughed as she pulled out a jar of peanut butter. "She said she knew you liked this brand. She felt bad that she didn't have anything more special to send you."

"*More* special?!" Esther took the jar from Chaya's hand and stared at it. It was exactly that same brand of peanut butter that she had just thrown away, only this one had a reliable hechsher on it! "Chaya, you're not going to believe this! This is the most special thing I could have gotten!"

As Esther told Chaya all about her day, she felt so close to Hashem. "He loves me so much, and just wants me to be happy! He planned this for me from when Chaya was in Montreal! I never even had to feel sad."

We all have special hashgachah from Hashem every moment of every day. He's always looking out for us, and He loves to make us happy.

Humble and Hidden

Rav Yitzchak Blazer was a brilliant student of Rabbi Yisrael Salanter. At the young age of 25, he became known as Rav Itzele Peterburger because he was appointed as the rav of St. Petersburg in Russia.

Rav Yitzchak was known for many things. He authored a few sefarim, headed Rav Yisrael Salanter's Kovno Kollel, and joined Rav Nosson Tzvi Finkel in leading the Slabodka Yeshivah. He was also known for his modesty. He worked as a house painter until Rav Yisrael Salanter told him to stop.

Once there was a meeting of many great rabbis in the city, where Rav Yitzchak was the rav. The great Beis HaLevi, Rabbi Yosef Dov Soloveitchik, also attended. During the meeting, the Beis HaLevi mentioned a difficult question that has been asked by his son, Rav Chaim Soloveichik.

The rabbanim began discussing the question, trying to come to an answer. The atmosphere was becoming heated as they tried to think of a solution. Rav Yosef Dov Soloveitchik presented a brilliant answer to the question. The rabbanim listened in awe. He then called on his son, Rav Chaim, to tell his answer.

Rav Chaim's answer was even more brilliant and complex than his father's. The rabbanim complimented him on his brilliance.

After the meeting, the Beis HaLevi returned home, but something was bothering him

"Rav Yitzchak Blazer was at the meeting. Everyone knows he is brilliant. We were all talking about my son Chaim's question. Why didn't Rav Yitzchok speak up even once. He must have some ideas! Why didn't he say anything?"

Rav Yosef Dov started pacing in his study. Then he stopped. He pulled a sefer from his bookshelf. It was the Pri Yitzchak, a sefer written by Rav Yitzchak Blazer. The Beis HaLevi opened it and flipped to the page that discussed the topic the rabbanim had been arguing about earlier. To his surprise, Rav Yitzchak had written the very same question in his sefer. Not only that, but he also had written both Rav Yosef Dov's and Rav Chaim's answers!

The Beis HaLevi smiled. "Rav Yitzchak is even greater than I thought before. This is true anivus, humility. He didn't want to take away any of the honor from me and Chaim, so he kept quiet."

Rav Yitzchak didn't need to hear praise from other people to make him feel important.

People don't like someone who boasts about his expensive vacation or the fancy Chanukah present his grandparents gave him. They respect someone who does good and does not brag about it.

Let's say you got a great mark on a test. You studied hard, you're very proud of yourself, and you want to tell everyone on the bus. You imagine all the kids on the bus will look at you with awe and respect. But you will earn much more respect by being humble.

It Pays to Trust

Brooklyn, New York, is still very busy and quite noisy at 8 p.m. It's dark out, but there are honking cars and lots of people in the stores. Some of this noise is generated in a small yeshivah filled with the sweet sounds of Torah learning. There are about a hundred people there. If you peeked inside, you would see that half of the people there are teenagers, and the other half are grown men. Each man is learning with a boy.

But tonight, there are two more people in the room. One of the yeshivah's rebbeim brought a special guest: one of the school's most generous donors, who gives lots of money to the yeshivah.

Mr. Goldman,* the donor, was impressed. "How do you get these boys to come back to the yeshivah every night after a long day? And even more importantly, how did you manage to get all these men to come and learn with them?"

Rabbi Kornbaum* smiled; his eyes lit up. "Learning is not easy for our boys. They need a little bit of extra help," he explained. "Every single night, these boys come to review what they have learned during the day. The men are happy to help them."

"This is amazing!" Mr. Goldman exclaimed. "I'm not sure what is more inspiring; the boys who come to learn every night, or the men who come to learn with them." He cleared his throat. "Here's what I want to do. I am going to give this yeshivah a big donation. I'm also going to give you extra money to raffle off for one of the tutors."

Rabbi Kornbaum shook his hand gratefully

That evening, Rabbi Kornbaum drew the raffle. He looked to see

---

* Not the real name.

who had won. It was Avrohom Klein,* a quiet, kind, and gentle man.

"Avrohom!" Rabbi Kornbaum called him excitedly. "We had a donor here earlier this evening and he donated money to raffle off for one of our tutors. You are the winner!"

Avrohom was shocked. "Rabbi Kornblum, I don't get paid for learning with one of the boys. I learn with my kid brother Menachem. My parents can't afford to pay for a tutor, so I said I would do it. When I told my wife, she suggested that I find someone else who would pay me to tutor. 'We really need the money,' she said. I told her not to worry. Hashem sees what I am doing. He is the One Who provides for us."

Later that night, Avrohom told the story to his wife, Shifra.* He made some quick calculations.

"Shifra!" he exclaimed. "You won't believe it. I won the exact amount of money that I would have made if I were being paid!"

Sometimes we think we know exactly what to do to get what we want. Many of those times, Hashem takes us on a different route that we would never have thought of. Hashem wants to remind us that He is the One running the world.

A Wonderous Wedding

Rav David Schechter boarded the bus to the Kosel. He went to the Kosel every day to daven and say Tehillim. When he came to the Wall, he tucked in a note for his daughter. She was getting married in a month, and he wanted to daven for the new couple's success.

While he was davening, he heard loud sobbing next to him. Someone was crying heavily, for a long time. Rav Schechter approached the man.

"What's wrong?" he asked. "Is there anything I can do to help?"

The man looked poor, his clothes were faded, and he needed a haircut. "I am marrying off my daughter next week, and I don't know how I will pay for it!"

"Don't worry," Rav David said soothingly. "Come with me, I will help you. "

They boarded the bus together, and he took the man to his home. He opened a drawer, took out the full amount that the man needed, and handed it to him. Rav Schechter had saved this money for his own daughter's wedding. He thought, *My daughter's wedding is in a month; his daughter's is next week. I still have time to get more money.*

The man thanked Rav Schechter emotionally and left. Rabbi Schechter checked his watch and realized it was almost time for him to leave for Minchah. Rabbi Schechter always tried to get there early.

As he walked to shul, there was a bounce in his step and a smile on his face. He opened the heavy door to the old shul and walked in. As he walked to his seat, he heard someone calling his name.

"Reb David, Reb, David!" He turned around. It was the great Rav Shlomo Goldman, the Zvhiller Rebbe! He took R' David's hand. "Please tell me what special mitzvah you did today!"

"Rebbi," Rav David replied with a twinkle in his eye, "if you can tell

that I did a special mitzvah, can't you tell which one I did?"

"Oh, Reb Dovid. Please just tell me what it was. If you do, I promise, I will find the time to teach you secrets of the Torah."

Rav Schechter shared what had happened that morning. "But how did you know?" Rav Schechter asked.

"When you walked in, I saw a special kedushah on you. There was a glow coming from you. You were so pure!" Rav Shloimke said.

Just then, Rav David Schechter's friend Reb Moshe walked in. He was very sad and had tears in his eyes.

"Rebbe," he said to the Zvhiller Rebbe. "My wife is so sick! Please, give me a berachah that she should live and be healthy."

Rav Shlomo looked at Rav Schechter. "It's better to ask Rav Schechter for a berachah. Right now, his words have more power than mine!"

Hashem is always protecting us, but when we do mitzvos, He gives us special powers and special protection.

Home Run

Mordechai was a sweet young boy who lived in a wonderful neighborhood. He had lots of friends with whom to play. Sadly, he became very sick. He was in a coma and couldn't even talk or see anyone.

Mordechai's friends and family tried to do whatever they could for his refuah sheleimah. They hosted berachos parties for the women, and shiurim for the men. The only ones who felt like they weren't doing anything for Mordechai's zechus were his classmates.

"We miss Mordechai the most," they said glumly. "What can we do?"

"I know!" Yosef said, "We could make a Tehillim group every day! We'll invite all the boys in the neighborhood, and we'll give everyone who joins a special treat!"

All the boys liked that idea, and so, the next day they started the Tehillim group. Every day it took place in someone else's house. Soon, Mordechai came out of his coma, but he was still very sick. The boys never missed a day of Tehillim.

Until the spring. As the weather began to get warmer and brighter, many of the boys left the Tehillim group, one by one. They wanted to play ball outside. Soon, there were only a few boys left in the group.

"Let's try our hardest to come every day," Yosef said to them. The other boys promised they would.

One day, there was a baseball game in the neighborhood. Only the very best players were on the teams. Yosef was one of them. Throughout the game, he kept checking his watch nervously. He didn't want to miss the Tehillim group, but the game was so important to him.

Soon it would be his turn to bat. He was swinging his bat as he waited. That's when he noticed it was time for the Tehillim group.

Yosef looked at his watch, and then back at the pitcher. He glanced back at the house where the group was meeting that day. He dug his bat into the sand, thinking.

At last, he dropped his bat and said, "Sorry, guys. I gotta run. I have my Tehillim group now." He ran off, and returned an hour later, when the game was long over.

Later that day, Yosef told his father what he had done.

"I'm so proud of you!" his father said. "That must have been a really hard decision to make. How about if we call Mordechai's family to tell them what you did? They will be so grateful for this zechus for Mordechai."

Yosef agreed, and soon, Mordechai's father was on the other line, listening to what had happened earlier that day.

"You're not going to believe this," Mordechai's father said emotionally. "Today, Mordechai had physical therapy and he did so well! Not only that, but the exercise he did was a game of baseball. He practiced swinging the bat and walking to first base, then second, then third, and finally, he walked home. It felt like a home run!

"It must be in your merit, Yosef," he said. "You gave up your baseball game and you helped Mordechai have a home run."

Yosef smiled. He felt as though Hashem was squeezing his shoulder encouragingly, saying, "*I see what you did! I am so proud of you.*"

Hashem always sees how hard a mitzvah is for us and He is proud of us when we make the right choice.

No Fights for the Flight

"Do we have everything?" Rabbi Nachum Silver* asked his wife Rivky, who was balancing her pocketbook on the top of her suitcase.

"Yes, I think so," she replied as she held the hand of their daughter, Shana.

The airport was very busy. Extra busy, it seemed. The Silvers were getting ready to leave Toronto where they had spent Shabbos visiting their parents.

"Passengers with young children may now board the flight," came the announcement over the loudspeaker.

"That's us!" Rivky said. "Let's go!"

As they walked to the line of people waiting to board, they were stopped by a flight attendant. "Are you Nachum Silver?" she asked.

"Yes, is there a problem?"

"Please come with me," she said as she led them to a side desk. "You are being placed on the next flight," she said. "This one is overbooked."

"But, but," Rabbi Silver sputtered, "but why? Why us? We were just called to board this flight!" Rabbi Silver was very agitated.

"Shh," Rivky whispered. "Don't raise your voice. It's a chillul Hashem."

Nachum turned to his wife. "You're right," he said.

They looked at the schedule for their new flight. They would have to wait an extra half hour, but they would be landing at an airport that was closer to their home.

As they sat down to wait, another flight attendant approached them. "May I see your tickets, please?" he asked.

Departures
AIR CANADA
Gate C12, LaGuardia
Flight 7480, 7:30 P.
ON TIME

After looking at them he said, "You can't get on this flight, it's full. You're going to have to wait until tomorrow."

Now Rabbi Silver was even more frustrated. "Tomorrow?!" he said incredulously.

"Shh," Rivky said.

"May I speak to your supervisor?" he asked in a calmer tone of voice.

The steward went to call his supervisor, and Nochum paced back and forth anxiously. While he was waiting, he noticed a familiar garment bag lying in a corner of the airport. "That's our suit bag!" he thought to himself. "If we had been on that first flight, we would've left it here!"

"Mr. Silver?" The supervisor had come. "I'm so sorry to hear about all the trouble you're having. I'll make sure that you get on the next flight tonight. And, because of all this inconvenience, I am going to give you $300 for each of you."

Rabbi Silver returned to his wife and daughter and told them the good news. As they settled onto the plane, a stewardess came over to them.

"I know that your original flight was going to land at a different airport, and your luggage is on that plane. But not to worry; we will have the luggage brought to your house for free. We are also going to pay for the car service to take you home from the airport."

Rabbi Silver looked at his wife. "Rivky, you were right. I should not have been so upset. Look, now we're landing at a closer airport, we didn't leave our garment bag behind, we were given an extra $900, they paid for our car service, and we won't have to wait in the airport for our luggage!"

Sometimes we are delayed. A flat tire, a missed flight, or maybe a series of red lights. But we must always remember that "Gam zu l'tovah!" Everything Hashem does is for the good. We may not know what it is, but there's always a good reason.

Mitzvah for Sale

Sarah Shain* read the "Apartments for Sale" column in the newspaper carefully.

"No, not that one… hmm, that one's too far… wait! What about this one?" She brought the paper to her husband, Reuven, to read.

"It's near my parents, it's ground level, and it's a good price. It won't last long; someone is sure to buy it."

They called the number in the advertisement and set up a time to see the apartment later that evening.

As they walked through the apartment, poking their heads in and out of every room and closet, Sarah and Reuven looked at each other.

"I think it's great," Sarah said quietly to her husband.

"Mmhmm," he agreed.

"So, we definitely want to take this apartment," Sarah told the woman who was showing them around, "but we don't have all the money just yet. I will pay you for it in three days when I have all the money. Is that alright with you? Can you save it for us until then?"

"If you're certain that you're going to buy it, then yes," the woman replied.

"Yes, we're absolutely certain," Sarah said.

"So then let's shake on it!" Sarah and the woman shook hands and promised to be in touch over the next few days.

Three days later, Sarah called up the woman exactly as she had promised. "I have all the money for you!" she said excitedly. "When would you like to meet?"

"Well… actually, I'm so sorry, but there was someone who came the

day after you. He was offering to pay me all the money for the apartment on the spot. I didn't want to lose that offer. I'm very sorry."

Sarah was shocked and oh-so-disappointed! "Who did you end up selling it to?" she asked sadly.

"Their names are Ben-Tzion and Shifra Kirzner," the woman replied.

Ben-Tzion and Shifra! Sarah thought, surprised. They were good friends with the Kirzners. This made Sarah feel even worse.

"You should bring her to Beis Din!" Sarah's coworker told her.

"You should let everyone know what they did!" her neighbor said, shaking her head.

"No," Reuven said later that night when Sarah told him what they had said. "We stay far away from fighting. Nothing good comes out of a machlokes. This is what Hashem wanted."

A few months later, while Sarah was at her desk working, the secretary called her to the phone urgently.

"It's my mother on the phone. She said her friend is looking to sell her home really quickly, and I think it's in the same area that you were looking for, near your parents, and for a great price!"

Sarah took the phone and listened. "60 Yechezkel Street?" she asked in shock. "That's right next door to my mother!"

Sarah and Reuven bought that home, and they were happier than they ever thought they could be!

When we give in and be mevater, we not only get special reward in Olam Haba! Sometimes we even get an extra bonus in this world, too.

An Experience

Rav Yisrael Salanter once had to travel to Paris, France. As he was walking down the streets, he started to feel very thirsty. Noticing a kosher café at the corner, he decided to stop in for a drink.

"May I please have a glass of water?" the tzaddik asked the waiter respectfully.

"Of course!" the waiter replied. "But you will need to take a seat at one of the tables and order your drink."

Rav Yisrael sat down and ordered water. When he was finished, he asked for his bill to pay for the water.

A few moments later, the waiter placed the bill on the table. When Rav Yisrael saw the amount, he was shocked!

"Why does it cost so much money for a simple glass of water?" he asked.

The waiter nodded patiently and explained. "You see, this bill is not just for the water you drank. You are paying for so much more than that. You are paying for the nice velvet-cushioned chairs, and for the beautiful view right outside the window. You are paying for the fine crystal glass in which the water was served, and for the beautiful surroundings in this café. You are paying to be served by me instead of having to get the water on your own. You are paying for the fine art displayed on the wall and for the cloth napkin right beside you. You are paying for the beautiful and relaxing music playing in the background and for the delicious scents in the air." He cleared his throat. "So, you see, the water is just one small part of the package. You are paying for the entire *experience* of drinking water in this beautiful place."

When Rav Yisrael Salanter heard this, his eyes lit up. He was eager to share this experience with his talmidim back home.

When he returned to Kovno, Lithuania, he told his students about his time in the café. "I now understand how we should feel when we make a berachah!" he said. "We would have to thank Hashem for food and drink even if we were eating in a dark, dirty dungeon. How much more so should we thank Him when we make a berachah in the comfort of our home! We are not thanking Hashem just for the water. We are thanking Him for everything around us — the bright sun, our loving family, our warm home, and our nice clothes. When we make that Shehakol, it's not just for the water — it's also for all the good things Hashem gives us along with it."

The next time you make a berachah, think of Rav Yisrael Salanter in Paris. Perhaps you are making Shehakol on a Shabbos treat. Thank Hashem for all the kosher treats you can choose from, your special Shabbos clothes, your friends you can share the treat with, your loving parents who bought it for you, and the comfortable chair you are sitting on. After all, we are not just saying thank You for the treat — we are saying thank You for the entire experience that comes along with it.

Loud and Clear

"So, you'll come?" Rabbi Alex Cohen asked Mike. "Our Shabbos meal will be at 7 o'clock Friday night."

Rabbi Alex Cohen always tried his best to bring not yet religious Jews closer to Hashem. A long time ago, he hadn't been religious himself, and his rebbi brought him close to Hashem. Now, he wanted to do the same for all of Hashem's children.

That Friday night, Rabbi Cohen and his wife, Rachel, waited for Mike. "I hope he shows up," Rabbi Cohen said. "I've been reaching out to him ever since I became the rav of this shul. I even prepared which zemiros to sing, and a special d'var Torah I'm sure he'll enjoy."

"I'm sure he'll show up," Rachel reassured him. She had prepared a delicious meal and a beautiful dessert. She even let the children stay up late in honor of their special guest.

At 7:15, Mike knocked on their door. Rabbi Cohen greeted him and showed him his seat. As Rabbi Cohen began to sing Shalom Aleichem, the Cohen's four-year-old daughter, Simi, piped up, "Ma, I'm so hungry!"

"Okay, sweetie, soon we will have the Shabbos seudah. Just a few more minutes," Rachel whispered to her daughter. Mike was watching them curiously.

"No, *now"* Simi insisted, loudly.

Rachel put her hand on Simi's shoulder to calm her down, but she only became more hysterical.

"Come, Simi," Rachel said softly. She took Simi by the hand and led her to the kitchen, but Simi just threw herself on to the floor and began kicking and screaming.

"I'm bringing the food now," Rachel said, desperately trying to make Simi happy.

Rabbi Cohen also spoke to her gently, but it didn't help. Simi just kept crying and shouting.

Rabbi Cohen felt so upset, but he tried not show it. He had thought of everything, trying to make this the very best experience for Mike.

It seemed that they had lost their chance. Rabbi Cohen was never even able to share his special d'var Torah.

Shortly after that Shabbos, Rabbi Cohen and his family moved to another city where he was asked to be the rav. One Shabbos, Rabbi Cohen was at a special event for ba'alei teshuvah. He was asked to speak, and when he stood up, he noticed a familiar face in the crowd. Could it be? Yes, it most definitely was Mike. Only now, he was wearing a kippah on his head.

After giving his speech, Rabbi Cohen walked over to Mike.

"Mike! Is this really you? I can't believe it! Tell me, what inspired you to become religious?"

"Well, Rabbi," Mike began, "do you remember when I came to your house for Shabbos?"

Rabbi Cohen definitely remembered, but he was hoping *Mike* had forgotten about the incident with Simi.

"Well, your little daughter was having a tantrum all through the meal, and I was watching. You and your wife were so calm! You didn't shout at her or make her feel bad for ruining the meal. When I saw that, I decided that I wanted to be like that! I wanted to be like you and your wife. And here I am."

Rabbi Cohen was shocked. "Do you realize how embarrassed I was when that happened?" he asked. "It's not only hashgachah that my daughter acted the way that she did to inspire you, but also that I met you here and was able to hear this story."

We have no idea who is watching us. We can always make a kiddush Hashem, and bring someone closer to their Father in heaven.

Double Donation

"I've been having headaches," Fred told his mother. She had come to visit him in Eretz Yisrael where he was learning. "And my stomach hurts, too."

Mrs. Betesh was concerned. "You are coming with me to a doctor," she said.

"His blood pressure is very high," the doctor said seriously. "And there are bad toxins in his blood. I'm almost certain the problem is with his kidneys and your son is going to need a kidney transplant."

The doctor ordered many tests and told Mrs. Betesh to come back in a few days. When she did so, he said, "I have serious news. Fred needs a new kidney. I put his name on the list of people waiting for one."

Mrs. Betesh was very worried. Everyone has two kidneys. A person can live and be healthy with only one kidney. They would have to find someone who was willing to give one of his kidneys to Fred. That person is called a "donor." But the donor's kidney would have to be exactly like Fred's. If everything is perfect, the doctors can remove a kidney from a healthy person and put it into the body of the sick person. Usually it takes a long time to find the right kind of kidney and a person who is willing to give it to the patient. The hospital would also need to do many tests.

Mrs. Betesh went home and started to daven. One rainy day, she went to a speech. After the speech, Mrs. Betesh was inside the building with other women, waiting for the rain to stop.

"Can everyone please do me a favor," Mrs. Betesh said. "My son is very sick. I would like to organize a berachos party, as a zechus for him to get better."

MT SINAI HOSPITAL
800-222-3111
07:46 PM
5/21
vtech

“I would love to!” said a girl, flipping to an empty page in her planner. “When should we do it?”

And so, Mrs. Betesh and this girl, Judy, arranged a berachos party for 150 women. There, they raised money for poor families in Eretz Yisrael. They had the pleasure of having Rebbetzin Ruchama Shain as their guest speaker.

That Shabbos, as the Betesh family were having their seudah, they heard the phone ring. It rang and rang until the call was picked up by the answering machine, which played the voicemail out loud in their home. “This is the hospital calling. Congratulations! We have a perfect kidney for you! You must bring Fred immediately.”

Since this was pikuach nefesh, a matter of saving Fred’s life, the Beteshes raced to the hospital.

“This kidney matches up in every way possible to you!” the doctors told Fred excitedly. They did the surgery, and eight days later, Fred left the hospital with a new kidney.

A few months later, Mrs. Betesh was speaking on the phone with Judy.

“You know the shidduch you suggested for me?” Judy asked. “It didn’t work out.”

“It didn’t? Hmm.” Mrs. Betesh thought a bit.

“Judy!” she exclaimed. “I think I have a wonderful shidduch idea for you!”

A few months after that, Fred and Judy were engaged. Mazel Tov! What hashgachah pratis! The girl who helped organize the berachos party to help Fred became his wife.

For a long time, every one of Fred’s donors did not work out. Hashem knew what was best for him and waited for the perfect kidney. Hashem knows what’s best for us, too. At every moment, everything is happening exactly the way it is supposed to.

Less Is More

Eliezer and Shevy Epstein lived in Gateshead, England. They had a beautiful family of seven children. All the children were special, but Shimmy was extra special.

You see, Shimmy had been born with a handicap. He could not communicate fully and do some things that other kids his age were able to do.

Shimmy was fast approaching his thirteenth birthday. His parents decided to make a small bar mitzvah celebration for him. They invited ten close couples to join them at their home for a seudah in honor of Shimmy's bar mitzvah.

During the seudah, the Rosh Yeshivah of Gateshead, Rav Leib Gurwicz, stood up to speak.

He said, "Each one of us is on this Earth for a different reason. Hashem has put us here to do our own unique job. Some of us are able to explain a very difficult piece of Gemara or run a successful business. Some of us are very talented, and some of us are very wise. Some of us have everything we need to do well in school — we are popular, look good, and carry on great conversations. Hashem gave us so many qualities and capabilities because we need to use them to accomplish a lot so our neshamos can finish our jobs in this world.

"Then there are some who are not as smart. Or those who were born with handicaps that make it impossible to do many things. These neshamos are already holy neshamos. They don't need to do so much to complete their jobs in this world. That's why Hashem didn't give them the talents and abilities that other people have. Maybe all they need to do is make a few berachos, or smile to people, or keep Shabbos. These neshamos need to do much less than other people's to make

it into Olam HaBa. The fewer capabilities someone is born with, the holier his neshamah is."

Rav Leib looked at Eliezer and Shevy Epstein and finished his speech by saying, "You are so fortunate! You were chosen to be the parents of this holy neshamah, and you get to have him in your family forever!"

The Epsteins were very moved, and thanked Rabbi Gurwicz from the bottom of their hearts.

A few days later, Eliezer took his son Shimmy to Eretz Yisrael to get a berachah from the Chazon Ish, the gadol hador. When they walked into his room, the tzaddik stood up! Eliezer looked around him to see who the Chazon Ish was standing up for. But there was no one there!

"Rabbi," he said, "please, you don't have to get up for me."

"I am standing for your son," the Chazon Ish corrected him. "He is one of the great neshamos of our generation, and he deserves my respect."

You may know someone who is in a wheelchair, or someone who has a speech problem. We have no idea how great people really are. Everyone deserves our respect, including those who seem to be less capable than we are.

Eye See You

It was Erev Shabbos Parashas Ki Seitzei. Tzvi Roth was ready. It was his bar mitzvah Shabbos, and he knew his leining and derashah perfectly. Tzvi's parents had invited over 100 guests, including his grandparents from Eretz Yisrael!

A few hours before Shabbos, Tzvi was at the hall with his parents adding some last-minute final touches.

"Tzvi, would you mind putting these vases on the tables?" his mother asked.

Tzvi carefully lifted each vase and placed it at the center of a table. As he was setting down the last vase, something sharp shot from the bottom of the vase and pricked him in his eye.

"Ow!' he exclaimed.

"Is everything alright, Tzvi?" his mother asked worriedly.

Tzvi was holding his eye, and his face was scrunched up in pain. "I think a piece of glass from the vase went into my eye," he whimpered.

Tzvi's father looked at his watch. It was 3:30 p.m. Quickly, he began to phone all the eye doctors in their area, but nobody answered. It was very close to Shabbos.

Mrs. Roth tried to call their pediatrician, but she kept getting a busy signal.

Seeing the commotion, the hall manager asked them what was wrong. Tzvi's parents told the man what had happened.

"I'm a member of Hatzoloh, let me have a look," he said. He took one look at Tzvi's eye and exclaimed, "He needs to get to a doctor right away! Take him to the emergency room."

Tzvi's parents looked at each other. The emergency room was a

45-minute drive away. If they were to go, there would be no way they could make it back in time for Shabbos. They would have to tell all their guests about the accident and put them up somewhere else for Shabbos. All the bar mitzvah planning and all of Tzvi's practice for his parashah would be for nothing.

"His health comes first," Tzvi's father said. Mrs. Roth nodded, and they all got into the Hatzoloh man's vehicle. As he started to pull out, Tzvi's mother thought for a moment.

"I'm going to try our pediatrician one more time," she thought out loud. Quickly, she dialed his number, and this time he picked up on the first ring.

"Dr. Brandon's office, how can I help you?"

Mrs. Roth told them the problem. "Bring him over. I'll see him right away."

They gave the Hatzoloh man directions, and a few minutes later, they pulled up at the doctor's office.

As Dr. Brandon peered into Tzvi's eye, Rabbi Roth told him, "It's his special moment this Shabbos. It's his bar mitzvah."

"Well, you're really lucky," the doctor said with a smile. "I am usually not the one who answers the phone, but I happened to be right next to it, so I picked up. Besides that, our phones are down and we're closed for the day but this phone was the only one that was still working! Your G-d was really looking out for you today."

He took another look at Tzvi's eye and said, "It seems like the piece of glass has already been flushed out of your eye. There's just a little scratch and it'll heal by itself. You're good to go."

Mrs. Roth thanked the doctor, and then looked up. "Thank You, Hashem," she said. "Your hashgachah is so clear that even the doctor was able to realize it!"

Hashem is always with us. He doesn't leave us for a second.

Learning and Yearning

Huda* was a good boy, with a good heart. He was great at many things. He was great at making friends, he was great at playing basketball, and he was great at building with wood. The one thing he wasn't great at was learning. No matter how hard he tried and studied, he was always behind the rest of his class.

Soon, Huda was entering eighth grade.

"Mommy," he said, worried, "which yeshivah will accept me? My grades are so low!"

"Don't worry," she said, "Hashem sees, and He will help us."

But sadly, all the yeshivos that Huda applied to said no. Huda was very discouraged. He sat in class and tried to participate, but he was feeling so down.

His rebbi noticed his sad face and decided to speak to the principal.

"Rav Landau," Huda's rebbi began, "we need to help our student, Huda Filer. He is a good boy, he tries very hard, but he has not yet been accepted to any yeshivah for next year."

Rav Landau stroked his beard. "I will call one of the yeshivos. I am close to the menahel, and he may do me a favor."

That evening, Rav Landau made his phone call.

"Yes, he seemed like a very sweet boy," the menahel said, "but how is he going to keep up with the other boys?"

Huda's principal replied. "So, he won't keep up with the other boys. But at least he'll be in a yeshivah! He is a good boy; he won't cause you any trouble. Please, accept him as a favor for me."

The menahel agreed.

The next year, Huda was overjoyed to be attending a regular

yeshivah with all his friends. He worked hard, and put in lots of effort.

Weeks and months passed, and would you believe, Huda was asking Tosafos's questions, and answering the Acharonim's answers. He quickly rose to be one of the best learners in the class, to everyone's surprise.

Soon, it was time to apply for Yeshivah Gedolah. This time, he had no problem getting accepted wherever he was tested! In fact, one rosh yeshivah even told him; "If you agree to come to our yeshivah, we will let you bring some other boys from your yeshivah who may not be as smart as you."

Huda was often asked how he managed to change so drastically and became able to understand Gemara so well. "Which tutor did you hire?" they wanted to know. "Which sefer did you use?"

Huda would just smile. But, at one point, Huda told his secret.

"Every night, when the beis medrash was empty, I would go up to the Aron Kodesh, and I would *cry.* I begged Hashem for the Siyata DiShmaya (help from Heaven) to understand the Gemara. That's how."

Hashem is always listening. He is waiting patiently and lovingly for us to turn to Him.

Food for Thought

Rabbi Shlomo Zalman Shtauber was an important part of the Tel Aviv Jewish community back in the mid-1970s. He would do everything he could to help his Jewish brothers keep the mitzvos as carefully as possible.

Rabbi Shtauber had a shoe store on 4 Yaffet Street in Jaffa, Israel. His store was right next to Abulafia, a famous Arab bakery. Every morning Reb Shlomo Zalman would have friendly conversations with the Arab bakery workers. He would also throw some wood chips into their oven. This would make sure that the bread would be Pas Yisrael for the Jewish people who bought from that bakery.

Every Pesach, all the Jewish bakeries in Eretz Yisrael would close. Abulafiah's bakery was open because he was not Jewish. Reb Shlomo Zalman noticed that some non-religious Jews were buying bread on Pesach from Abulafia. He was overcome with sadness.

The next year, Reb Shlomo Zalman thought of a plan.

"Sayeed, my friend!" he called to the owner of the bakery. "It hurts me so much to see my Jewish brothers buy bread from you on Pesach. I want to make a deal with you. You tell me how much money you make on Pesach. I will pay you that amount to close your bakery for Pesach."

Sayeed thought about it. "It's a lot of money," he said. "It's my most profitable week of the whole year!"

"Please," Rabbi Shtauber begged with tears in his eyes. "It will be good for you. You work so hard all year. You could use that week to take a vacation."

A vacation sounded very good to Sayeed, and he agreed. They wrote a contract saying that Sayeed agrees to close his Abulafia bakery on

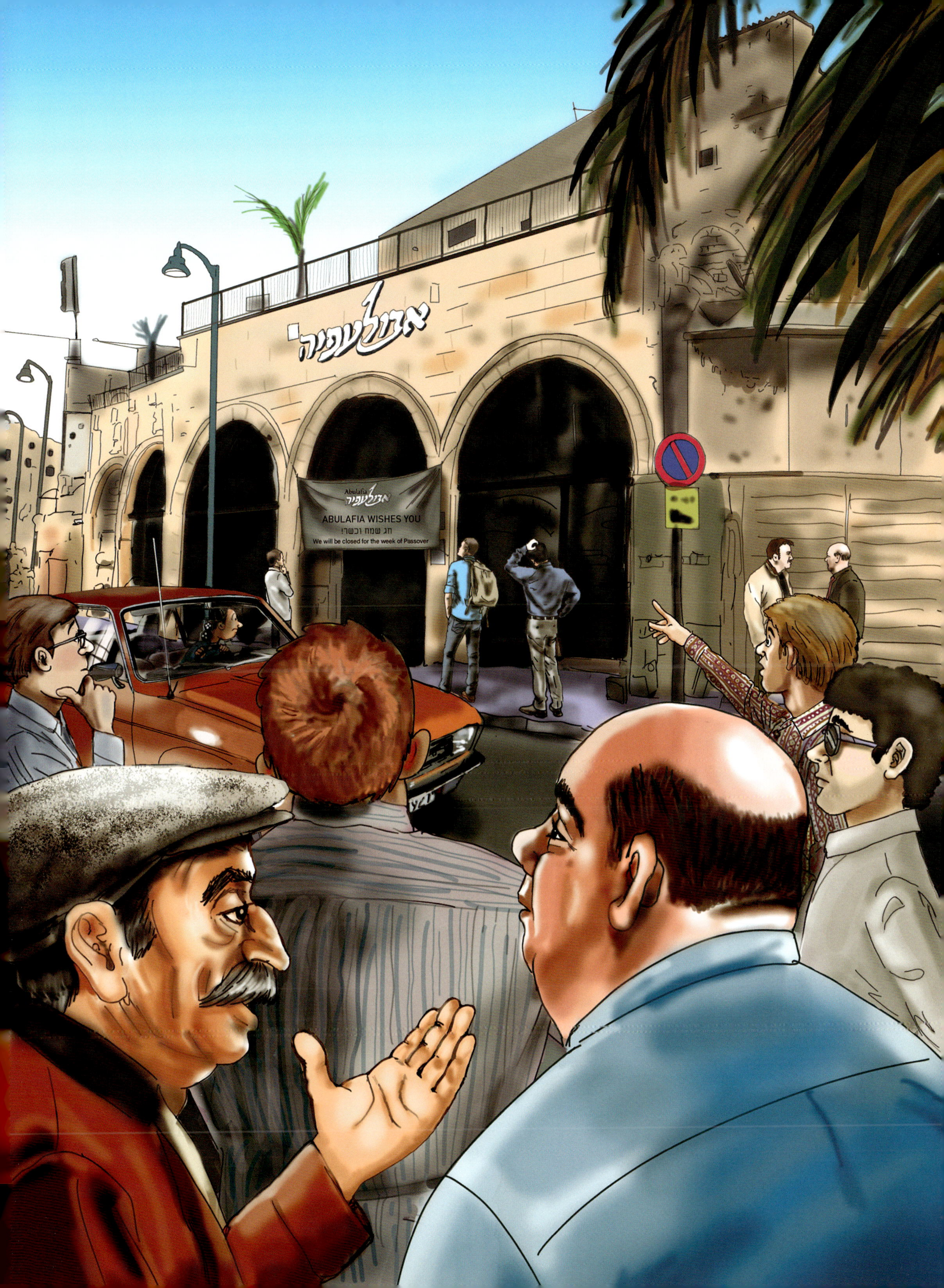
אבולעפיה
Abulafia
ABULAFIA WISHES YOU
חג שמח וכשר!
We will be closed for the week of Passover

Pesach, and Rabbi Shtauber would pay him all the money he would have made that week.

It was a huge sum of money. Reb Shlomo Zalman had no idea how he would get that much, but he knew he had to do whatever he could to prevent Jews from eating chametz on Pesach.

That Pesach, while Sayeed was on vacation with his family, his customers pulled up to his store. Imagine their surprise when they saw the sign on the bakery:

"Abulafia wishes you a Chag Kosher V'sameach! We will be closed for the week of Pesach."

This arrangement continued for six years. Each year, they would write up the agreement, and each year, Reb Shlomo Zalman Shtauber would pay Sayeed Abulafia a huge amount of money.

The sixth year, Sayeed said, "Rabbi, you can't imagine the blessing and profits we've had over the past six years. We've made so much more money than we ever did! I think it's in the merit of closing the bakery on Pesach. Your G-d has paid me back. I really don't need your money anymore. I will keep closing my bakery on Pesach and you don't have to pay me."

By now, both Rabbi Shtauber and Sayeed have passed away. But Sayeed's grandson who now owns the bakery keeps the same tradition. And every Pesach, the Abulafia Bakery is closed.

*It is a big Kiddush Hashem when the nations of the world see the hand of Hashem. It is an even bigger Kiddush Hashem when **we** get to see Hashem's hashgachah.*

Fun for All

It was noisy downstairs. The sound of children playing, arcade games beeping, and rides whirring filled the air. Steven Sutton* was in his office, where it was quiet. He is the owner of an indoor amusement park. It had games, a climbing gym, several rides, and lots of prizes. Camps and schools loved to come there. Families would make birthday parties. Steven even has a kosher pizza store on site!

The phone rang. He leaned back in his chair as he answered the call. "Hello. You've reached Action Park. How can I help you?"

It was the director of a boys camp that had booked the entire amusement park four months earlier. They had scheduled for 300 boys to come that week, but they wanted to cancel.

"You want to cancel?" Steven asked, making sure he heard correctly.

"Yes," replied the camp director. "Something came up and we need to cancel."

I will lose a lot of money from this, Steven thought to himself. Aloud, he said, "Okay, I will cancel your reservation for Wednesday." Steven hung up the phone, feeling a bit upset.

"Hashem is in charge of parnassah," he reminded himself. "And I can be proud of myself that I did not yell at the man on the phone."

Steven was already starting to feel better, so he made his way downstairs to check on the amusement park.

As he passed a family whose children who just won 1,000 tickets, he slapped them high fives. He saw another child looking in his pocket for more tokens and he handed him some tokens free of charge. He helped a young girl who was looking for her other shoe. He gave big smiles to all of his staff, and already, he was feeling a whole lot better.

As he climbed the stairs to go back to his office, the phone was

Action Park
EMERGENCY
AUGUST 2021
Sunday
Monday
Tuesday
Wednesday
Thursday
Friday
Saturday
Canon
Call
Danny
Snapple

ringing. He ran up to his desk and picked up the phone. "Hello? Action Park, how can I help you?"

"Hi," came the woman's voice on the other end of the phone, "I am the director of a girls camp here, and I need to make a last-minute reservation for this Wednesday. Would you happen to have that day available?" she asked.

"This Wednesday!" Steven exclaimed. "What hashgachah!" Steven would not rent out the park to both boys and girls camps at the same time. Since the boys camp had canceled, the girls were able to come instead. "Yes, I have that slot available for you. How many girls are in your camp?"

"Well, we have 300 girls, so we would need to rent the entire park. We also want to buy 3200 tokens for them," the woman said.

"Thank You, Hashem!" Steven said out loud. The woman at the other end was surprised, but Steven didn't care. "Thank You, Hashem!" he said again.

Steven marveled at the hashgachah. Not only did he have a camp to fill the slot, they would even be buying lots of tokens.

Every morning when Steven walks into his amusement park , he thinks of this story, and he knows that Hashem is always looking out for him.

We don't always see how something is for our best when it happens. We should remember how much Hashem loves us. Then, we can trust that it's all for the best.

Joy and Love for All

Motke Zubitzki had several beautiful daughters in shidduchim, each one an amazing ba'alas middos. The only problem was that Motke was poor. Very poor. And no one wanted to do a shidduch with his family because he could not share in the expenses.

One day, Motke was listening to the rav's shiur. He got an idea. The rav was saying that Hashem pays us back if we do things for others. So, Motke decided that he was going to share in his friends' happy occasions. Maybe that would be a zechus for his daughters.

A week later, Motke's neighbor invited him to his daughter's wedding. Motke put on his best suit and shoes and went to the hall. "Mazel tov! Mazel tov!" he said with a big smile, shaking his neighbor's hand. Usually this would be when Motke would leave, but this time he stayed.

He sat at a table with several people he didn't know. He listened to their conversation.

"I heard that he fired all the workers from his store," a man said. "That Abramowitz!"

"Yes," another one added in, "I heard that he knew that his store was going to close, but he didn't tell his workers, and now they are all out of a job! He is such a mean person. He kept the information to himself so that they could not look for other jobs."

As Motke heard all this lashon hara about a Mr. Abramowitz, he looked around the table. It seemed like everyone was listening and no one was stopping these men. Motke was a shy man, but lashon hara? This was such a big aveirah that he felt he had to speak.

"Do you realize what you are saying?" he interrupted. "You have no right to talk about anyone like that. This is lashon hara! Did you

ever think that maybe Mr. Abramowitz didn't tell his workers because he was hoping he could keep the store open? Did you ever think that maybe Mr. Abramowitz might be planning to give those workers a job in another store? No? So then don't go around saying terrible things about him."

The table grew very quiet, and the conversation ended.

No one had noticed, but Mr. Abramowitz was sitting near their table, listening to the conversation. When the wedding was over, he went over and asked someone about Motke. When he heard that he had daughters who needed to get married, he went to Motke's house for a visit.

"You know, R' Motke, I heard everything they were saying about me at the wedding. Each word was like a needle in my heart. And then you spoke up. Everything you said about me was true. Thank you from the bottom of my heart." He cleared his throat.

"I heard you have a daughter in shidduchim. I have a son in shidduchim. I have been so afraid to let him get engaged to anyone because I am afraid that all they want is my money. But I know you are sincere. What do you say to this shidduch?"

Motke's daughter and Mr. Abramovitz's son met and within a few weeks they were engaged. Mr. Abramowitz also gave Motke a good job in his business, and he finally had enough money to marry off his other daughters. Over the next few years, each of them found her match and married.

> *In just a few seconds, Motke's life changed for the better. "Yeshuas Hashem k'heref ayin," Hashem's help comes as fast as the blink of an eye. And the way we act is quickly rewarded.*